Body Aware Grieving

A Fitness Trainer's Guide to Caring for Your Health During Sad Times

Margo Rose

Margo Rose/PHT Press
29 Orinda Way, #881
Orinda, CA 94563
BodyAwareGrieving.com

ISBN-13: 978-0692459188

Contents:

Healing with Cultures Around The
World

Introduction

Welcome!

If you've picked up this book it's likely that you or someone you care about is going through a difficult time. Changes like losing a loved one or pet, facing an injury or setback, the end of a relationship or career are likely to have almost anyone feeling scared, sad and confused for a while.

The goal of this book is to look for ways to get through hard times like these as smoothly and safely as possible. Sometimes we can't stop sad events from happening, but we can become *more prepared and less scared* in our response to them.

We all want to feel that we are able to handle the various changes, challenges and disappointments we encounter skillfully. Even when faced with circumstances beyond our control, we want to know how to take good care of ourselves and the people we love.

Often we are busy with trying to earn or manage money, care for our children, parents and pets--sometimes all at once. Many of us want to create exciting, stable relationships and still have time to develop our personal passions. Of course we also need to exercise, take care of our health and find ways to stay vibrant and active as we age.

With so many priorities in our lives, we are often ill-prepared for emergencies and problems when they arise. Especially for those of us who are already busy, an unexpected event like caregiving for a family member or romantic break-up may lead us to feel overwhelmed and stressed.

Most of the setbacks that happen in our lives including losses to grieve, financial problems, relationship issues, caring for our health as we age or if we become ill, are actually common around the world and throughout history. Our goal is to learn how to best master these basic human experiences, now...within today's fast-paced lifestyles.

Body Aware Grieving is a system of self-care designed for people who want to become wiser and more talented at handling difficult situations.

Whatever troubles we are currently facing, we can explore how to pay attention to our emotions, take care of our health and still think clearly enough to get through tough transitions skillfully.

We can learn to become more calm, confident and optimistic, inspired to make our current and future lives as enjoyable as possible!

Most of all, we need to be patient and kind to ourselves and the people around us as we go through difficult times and into more joyful ones.

How to use this book
Read the information offered here in any order that you prefer. See which sections seem most beneficial and appealing to you. That said, high priority in any circumstance is to protect your health which is why I have placed the chapters devoted to injury reduction near the beginning.

In the first parts of this book, I have provided ideas and suggestions. The last section of the book has blank pages where you are invited to write, draw or add images so you can begin making your own Healing Action Plan!

At the back of the book I have included space for you to take notes, expand your ideas, include photos of loved ones, quotes that you find inspiring or additional information that guides you in a direction of your choice.

Develop and grow your own Body Aware Grieving plan whichever way is most convenient: on a computer or phone, in a journal, as a mural on a wall in your house... Become as inspired and creative as you'd like!

If you or someone you are caring for is currently suffering with emotions that are hard to handle I recommend checking out the section called 10 Actions of Healing. The goal is to find activities that can improve how you are feeling and functioning in as little as 15 minutes!

I've shared my examples of how to utilize the 10 Actions of healing within that chapter. You can add your own healing activities for each of the 10 Actions of Healing in the Your Healing Action Plan section at the back of the book.

Don't feel limited by the amount of space provided in this book. The more favorite activities you can think of, the better! Over time, you can add new options and take out any that you try but do not find beneficial.

At the end of each chapter, written in italics, are *Questions to Consider* intended to help you further explore and personalize the main ideas. There is no right or wrong way to approach these questions. Answer as many or few of them as you find interesting. If you'd like, use the extra pages at the back of this book to explore your own answers to the end-of-chapter questions.

My Story

I have been a personal and group fitness instructor for over 15 years. My specialties include:

- Injury reduction; learning to avoid accidents, injuries, and illnesses whenever possible.
- Senior wellness; ways to stay fit and active while adjusting to the changes that happen to our bodies over time.
- Comfort-focused fitness; moving with ease and enjoyment.
- Body Aware Grieving; practical ways to care for your health during times of loss, stress or disappointment

I've been asked why I became so interested in healing from loss. My education about grief got a big start when I went through a period with multiple changes at the same time. Sometimes life just happens like that...

A romantic partner passed away suddenly the same week I was moving back to my hometown to help take care of my mother who was losing her battle with cancer. For a while I was completely in shock and it was really overwhelming. Eventually I was able to create effective ways to function well, even when I was upset. It was exciting to emerge from those stressful experiences and I was proud of myself having made it through those hard times!

Then, more challenges arrived all together. Within a four year period, my father passed away from cancer, we lost my little sister to suicide, two aunts and both of my pet bunnies also passed away. I was working as a fitness trainer and while I was struggling to adjust to those losses, the economy got worse suddenly and half my clients cancelled their sessions.

Even though I was sad and scared, I managed to handle my responsibilities pretty well, but then I started to sink into a depression which became its own problem. Who is going to hire a fitness trainer who has low energy and an attitude like, "Why bother? We're all going to die anyway..."

I needed to learn how to take care of myself better, so I began to be very practical. My focus was on getting through each hour of each day as well as possible. I would talk to myself, sometimes out loud, and say, **"Okay, I need 3 things right now. I need to protect my health, recover from these losses and get stronger. How can I do these three things?"**

I ended up creating what I call: Body Aware Grieving, practical ways to care for your health during times of loss, stress or disappointment.

The goal is to become more organized and efficient, even when dealing with strong emotions.

I have been inventing the Body Aware Grieving system of self-care for almost twenty years.

This book, A Fitness Trainer's Guide to Caring For Your Health During Sad Times is an introduction to these ideas. There is much more useful information to share! I am also creating healing care kits for specific problems, a radio show, live events, comfort-focused fitness exercise videos and a website, www.BodyAwareGrieving.com where we can learn from one another.

The information in this and my upcoming books is designed to be compatible with other healthcare systems and practitioners including:
Grief counselors
Hospice providers
Suicide prevention advocates
Mental health practitioners
Veteran and military support programs
Healing arts: therapeutic massage, yoga, meditation etc.
Services for seniors
Substance abuse recovery programs
Religious organizations
Medical hospitals and rehabilitation clinics

One of my hopes is that we can improve communication and cooperation among caregivers, caregiving organizations and health care practitioners; so that individuals going through mental and physical challenges can use the range of healing services they need in a more organized manner.

My experience is based on being a fitness trainer and I'm not offering, nor trying to replace, any of the services listed above. If you or people you are caring for would benefit from professional services, I encourage you to reach out to those providers.

After considering everything I've discovered these past years from my own experiences and while working with clients, my primary goal is to summarize for you the most useful information possible.

The first **Practical Healing Technique** I will share is **10 Actions of Healing:**
Hibernate
Hydrate
Commemorate
Create
Liberate
Donate
Celebrate
Relate
Contemplate Fate
Rejuvenate

If you are unsure how to begin your own journey towards feeling better, choose which Actions of Healing most appeal to you and begin inventing your own healing action plan today!

10 Actions of Healing

10 Actions of Healing

Getting through hard times, adjusting to losses and becoming stronger often involves experimentation. Perhaps you don't always know what to do next or which types of assistance to ask for when struggling with a problem. For that reason, having a wide variety of possible ways to improve your circumstances is useful.

If you tend to be a very busy person, especially if much of your energy is spent caregiving for others, it is essential to find more time in your schedule to focus on your own needs. **An important 'action' to start with, is to look for ways is minimize your responsibilities to others and prioritize your own relaxation and opportunity to heal.**

Try to have an open and hopeful attitude. No matter what is happening in your life, you are not 'stuck'. Below is a list of potentially beneficial activities called **10 Actions of Healing**. The idea is that choosing an activity from any of these categories, in whatever order you prefer, may improve how you are feeling and functioning.

Hibernate
Can you improve the quality or quantity of rest you are getting?

Hydrate
Are you taking in enough healthy fluids and juicy foods?

Commemorate
What or whom are you missing now?

Create
Can you express your feelings with art, music, writing or movement?

Liberate
Which old ideas or items are no longer necessary?

Donate
Can you help others in a way that is uplifting to you?

Celebrate
How can you have more fun and enjoyment?

Relate
Who is currently most caring and helpful?

Contemplate Fate
What has the most meaning to you?

Rejuvenate
Who can you become now?

This chapter is filled with examples of healing options that I have provided and at the back of the book are blank pages where you are encouraged to begin inventing your own Healing Action Plan.

There are three main advantages to personalizing the 10 Actions of Healing with your own favorite ideas and activities.

1. It can be empowering to realize that even during upsetting situations you can still make choices that improve your well-being.

2. No matter how busy your schedule, it is possible to devote at least 5-15 minutes at a time to activities that are nurturing and consoling.

3. Your concerns and circumstances are unique. 10 Actions of Healing is a way to discover which activities and people are most uplifting and beneficial to you personally.

Especially if you have a busy schedule, it can be helpful to list healing options

according to how long they may take
to accomplish.

How much time is needed for each
'action'?

- 5-15 minutes
- 1-5 hours
- 1 Day
- 10 or more Days
- Ongoing

Also customize each idea by taking
note of how much it might cost:

- Free
- Under $25
- $25-$100
- Over $100

Also consider with whom you may
want to share each activity:

- Alone
- Friends or family
- A romantic partner
- Your pet or other animal
- Groups of people who share
  your interests, either in person
  or online
- Religious organizations
- Professional providers

If you are not feeling well or are
experiencing a high level of stress, it

may be harder to think of activities that are fun, comforting or inspiring. You can ask people who have known you at different phases of your life what they remember you enjoying and feeling purposeful doing. Think about hobbies you've loved, places you've been or adventures you've always wanted to try!

HIBERNATE
- Sleep is one of the natural medicines of grief recovery. Are you getting enough rest?
- How can you increase the quality and or quantity of sleep you are getting? Being sleep deprived can make it harder to think clearly, manage stress and move safely.
- Do you like to nap? Even if you do not actually sleep, it can be very refreshing to relax for at least 20 minutes each day.

Hibernate action examples:
5-15 minutes
Buy an eye 'mask' that blocks out light in any environment

1-5 Hours

Look online or at a library for information about reducing insomnia

1 Day

Create a 'day of rest' with favorite relaxing activities and minimal responsibilities. Try to do it every week!

10+ days

Experiment with pre-bedtime rituals to create more peaceful sleep. Keep a journal about which choices are most successful.

Ongoing

Avoid answering the phone or beginning stressful discussions after 8pm

HYDRATE

- Are you taking in enough fluids and healthful juicy foods?
- Do you have the nutrition that you need to keep your moods stable and body energized?

- Early signs of mild dehydration may include: headache, dry skin, decreased urine volume, unexplained tiredness, constipation, dizziness or insomnia. Are you experiencing any of these symptoms?

Hydrate action examples
5-15 minutes
Choose a healthy, high moisture food or beverage to enjoy

1-5 hours
Research appealing food and beverage options that are low in sodium, sugar, alcohol and caffeine

1 Day
Attend a class or workshop about healthful cooking or juicing

10+ Days Create a "bar" at home and experiment with creative sparkling waters, teas, herbs and flavorings

Ongoing Buy a juicer and drink at least one vegetable blend beverage a day

COMMEMORATE

- Who or what are you missing right now?
- What are you thinking about that is bringing up feelings of sadness or loss?
- Which rituals or activities will help you acknowledge these important people and experiences in a way that is satisfying to you?

Commemorate action examples

5-15 minutes Look at a photo, listen to a song or touch a symbolic item that reminds you of your favorite memories

1-5 hours Plan how to spend an upcoming special date like a memorial, anniversary, or holiday

1 Day Visit a place or person who reminds you of a special time in your life

10+ Days Do one activity each day that would make a loved one you are thinking of proud

Ongoing Stay in contact with people who have an important experience in common with you

CREATE
- Are you attracted to using music, painting, art, photography, writing or video to express what you are experiencing?
- Perhaps you don't want to actually do these activities yourself. Can you can find music, books, artwork, movies or live events that match your current mood?
- Dreams are a source of creativity also. Do you remember having dreams about the person you are thinking about or change you are going through?

Create action examples
5-15 minutes Imagine which sound, image, color or animal is most like your current mood

1-5 hours Tell a story using art: writing, music, photography, video, or movement

1 Day Build or fix something! Work on a tree house, bookshelf, garden or other project

10+ Days Learn a new skill or improve a current talent

Ongoing Find ways to express your true feelings at least 10 minutes each day without hurting yourself or anyone else

LIBERATE

- Are there ideas, activities or people in your life that aren't necessary or beneficial anymore?
- Are there any worries or responsibilities you can now be relieved from?
- Especially if you have been caregiving for a pet or loved one who has passed away or if you have been focused on a job,

goal or romance that has changed, your life may be different now. Are you carrying any guilt, shame, worry or regret you can let go?

Liberate action examples
5-15 minutes Think of three responsibilities you no longer have, for example, take Dad to the doctor

1-5 hours Remove items from home, garage, car or office that are not being used

1 Day Hire a professional or ask a friend to do a task you've been postponing

10+ Days Write down one self-criticism or complaint per day then tear up burn, bury or delete it

Ongoing If you are struggling with regrets or guilt ask yourself, "What am I going to accept about this situation? What can I change about my current or future behavior?"

DONATE

- Can you find a sense of empowerment and joy in helping others?
- Would you enjoy being of service by sharing a bit of your time, wisdom, energy or money in a way that will brighten someone's life?
- Are there physical belongings in your life that are no longer useful to you that you can give away?

Donate action examples
5-15 minutes Contribute to a favorite person, group, organization

1-5 hours Volunteer in person to help a project you find inspiring

1 Day Get certified in CPR and first aid to become more prepared to help in an emergency

10+ Days Learn how to assist with seniors, children, animals, suicide reduction or addiction recovery

Ongoing Smile and make eye contact with people in public...your kindness may become the best part of someone's day

CELEBRATE
- How can you reward yourself for overcoming the hard times by looking for more opportunities to celebrate and have fun?
- Which favorite activities and people do you most enjoy?
- Are there new adventures you feel ready to try?

Celebrate action examples
5-15 minutes Find a joke, video, picture or person that makes you laugh

1-5 hours Enjoy an excellent meal in a beautiful location

1 Day Do at least three of your favorite activities in one day

10+ Days Choose an exciting new goal or hobby

Ongoing Think of 5 things you are grateful for each morning and night

RELATE

- Who is currently most beneficial and kind to you?
- Who helps you feel good about yourself?
- How can you connect more often and more deeply with the individuals and groups that support your goals?

Relate

5-15 minutes Tell someone how you are feeling right now, write it out if that is easier for you

1-5 hours Organize a list of important people in your life and make sure they have each other's phone numbers and email addresses

1 Day Meet at least one new person, locally or online

10+ Days Notice how you feel, emotionally and physically, when you have contact with each of your friends and family members.

Ongoing Increase the amount of contact you have with the people you enjoy most. Visit, write, or call your favorite people more often.

CONTEMPLATE FATE

- What has the most meaning to you now?
- After a major change or loss, is your way of looking at yourself or the world different now?
- When facing hard times, which ideas or people can help you restore a sense of hope?

Contemplate Fate
5-15 minutes Take 10 or more slow, deep breaths in a comfortable position with eyes open or closed

1-5 hours Attend a religious service, perhaps of a faith other than your own

1 Day Spend a day, or part of one, without speaking

10+ Days Find a teacher, mentor, respected friend or religious guide and ask them for advice

Ongoing Be in nature at least 30 minutes a day, look around with curiosity

REJUVENATE
- Who can you become now?
- How can you utilize your newly gained wisdom and talents to be happier and more powerful than before?
- Can you be curious and optimistic about the new opportunities that may be possible for you?

Rejuvenate
5-15 minutes Get a new view! Clean a window, mirror, electronic screen, or glasses

1-5 hours Exercise carefully then get a massage, facial, or manicure

1 Day Take a mini-vacation! It can be

relaxing, educational or adventurous based on your mood

10+ Days Choose an interesting new goal or hobby

Ongoing Explore ways to use your newly gained wisdom, courage and empathy to become the best person you've ever been

Remember there is an area for you to invent your own 10 Actions of Healing ideas at the back of this book!

Protecting Your Health

PROTECTING YOUR HEALTH:

3 Types of Injury Reduction
The biggest first step towards healing is learning how to avoid creating new problems and setbacks. It is easier to start getting better when you find ways to stop getting worse!

1. Injury reduction begins with avoiding physical accidents. When people have strong emotions like anger, shock or sadness, it becomes harder to move safely and think clearly.

We can improve our chances of avoiding accidents by slowing down whenever we are not functioning at full capacity. That means being more careful when walking, especially down stairs or on uneven surfaces. We need to pay extra attention when doing physically challenging activities like using a knife, climbing a ladder or lifting a heavy item.

It is especially important to be aware of how well we are doing before starting to drive. It is not fair to ourselves or the other people on the road to be driving a vehicle when we are not emotionally or physically capable of doing so safely.

Don't take on any extra challenges or responsibilities if you are tired, dizzy or distracted by strong emotions. Slow down physically and reduce how busy you expect yourself to be in order to stay safer!

2. The next step of injury reduction is lowering the chance of stress-related habits and illnesses. Our goal is to find healthy ways to reward and console ourselves! When we are feeling stressed, busy or upset it is common to misuse food, alcohol or drugs in a manner that may have negative consequences.

Stress-related setbacks can also happen when people are holding in or trying to ignore their emotions in a way that is hurtful to them. This can lead to symptoms including sleeplessness, muscle or joint pain, headaches, depression, anxiety problems and even suicidal thoughts. Physical illness or disease is harder to heal from when accompanied by emotional distress.

We can look for a wider range of simple, personalized ways to provide ourselves with pleasure and reduce our need for less healthy habits. It could be something as simple as watching a funny video, calling a friend or playing a favorite song. We need to find ways to express how we feel and lower our stress level however works best for our individual circumstances and preferences.

3. A third part of injury reduction is avoiding what I refer to as a 'multiplication of problems'. For example, if we are dealing with tension or fighting at home, our strong emotions or fatigue might lead us to make more mistakes at our job which could lead to financial trouble. Or if we are feeling anxious or resentful we may behave in an impatient or unkind way to our friends or family and create new problems in those relationships.

It is important to isolate each challenge to keep it from expanding into other parts of our life and causing new troubles. **One useful technique is to separate each part of the day with a relaxing, uplifting activity that is at least ten minutes long.** It can be hugely beneficial to take even a few moments to become calmer before and after each major part of the day such as beginning and ending work, before and after driving, connecting with friends or family, going to sleep and waking.

3 Types of Injury Reduction-- Questions to consider

What is one change you are willing to make that could help reduce your chances of injury? Make a list of five or more activities that you find calming and enjoyable including some that can be done in 10 minutes or less. Can you do at least two of these activities each day for a week and see how you feel?

Knowing when we need help

Even when we do not realize that we are being affected by stress, sadness or anger, our bodies will often display symptoms that let us know we are functioning at less than our full capacity.

Common signs that we need to take better care of ourselves may include stomach or digestive issues, back or neck pain, fatigue, sleeplessness, muscle tension, dizziness, inability to concentrate, mood swings, incessant crying, under or over-eating, overuse of medication, drugs or alcohol, getting colds or the flu repeatedly.

Each person going through a loss will experience it differently. Signs of stress or grief can be subtle, at least at first, and may become more extreme if they are not addressed. **One of the most important moments in healing can occur when we realize that we have a problem that is not passing on its own.**

Instead of feeling 'weak' when we realize we may need help, it can be exciting to explore the questions: "What can I do to get through my current situation with the least amount of extra suffering?" "Which people, products, services, professionals, or organizations are available and useful to me?" Questions like these can begin to lead us towards feeling and functioning better as soon as possible!

Here is a story from my own life. The most dramatic response to stress and loss I have experienced was when my father was ill. My father had enjoyed exceptional physical health until age 70 when he was diagnosed with pancreatic cancer. After he underwent surgery to slow the progression of his disease, I was grateful to be able to work with him as a fitness trainer to help him regain his strength.

At first he made amazing progress. Then his health suddenly worsened and he lost 15 pounds in one week! I then understood for the first time, that my father was going to die from his illness, probably within a short time. For the next few weeks I could not stop crying. I would literally be sobbing myself to sleep and then wake up with new tears in my eyes before they were even open.

After a while, I realized that these extreme signs of distress were taking over. It was incredibly hard to go to work or eat healthfully which quickly resulted in financial problems and becoming physically weak. I felt exhausted, worried, sad and scared.

There are times when any one of us could need assistance, and I was trying not to become any more despondent. It is hard to say what is a "normal" amount of grief, but I began telling my family, friends and eventually a therapist what was happening so they could provide more support and help me figure out how to get through each day.

Physical limitations like being sick or injured are easier to see, but sometimes we need help with emotional and mental troubles as well. **Instead of using energy to fight the fact that we are struggling, it can be more efficient to start figuring out which friends, organizations or professionals will be able to help us improve how feel and function.**

Knowing When We Need Help--
Questions to consider
What is the most challenging part of your day? Why? Can you think of two people or organizations that may be able to make this current problem easier?

What does it mean to be "Body Aware"?

Figuring out how to answer the question, "What does it mean to be body aware?" hasn't been easy. The general idea is that we have five basic senses: sight, hearing, touch, taste and smell. Some people have all five of the senses functioning very well, while others of us may have lost full use of these capabilities over time, due to an accident, illness or limitation from birth.

In order to move safely, we want to take in as much information about our surroundings as possible and integrate this information as quickly as we can.

Here is an example, the other day I was going for a walk and there was a big crack in the sidewalk that I didn't see in advance. My ankle started to turn in a way that would have likely resulted to a sprained ankle and probable fall onto the cement.

Instead, my sense of 'touch' noticed that part of my foot was no longer in contact with the sidewalk and my body responded with quick reflexes in a way that helped me regain my balance and avoid falling.

I was relieved and happy to have avoided a serious injury and realized that faster response times to danger is one of the biggest advantages of body awareness!

If there is a fire nearby, the sooner we see the flames or the smell smoke the quicker we can begin choosing what to do to improve the situation. When we are walking or driving as soon as we hear a car honking or siren from an emergency vehicle, we can look around and see what we need to do to become safer. If we are eating and notice by smell or taste that the food is no longer fresh, this information can stop us from eating an amount that might make us sick.

When we use our senses to notice information about the environment around us, we can make better choices about our own well-being. Body awareness is one of the most important tools that help us with injury reduction.

We can also improve our quality of life by paying attention to our senses. If we sit down to a delicious meal we can fully savor the smell, taste and feel of the food. During a walk outside we can notice if the temperature feels good on our skin and if the views we are looking at are interesting or beautiful.

When we talk with a person we care about, we can connect more deeply by hearing the tone of their voice and seeing which emotions they are expressing in their face or body.

If there are so many advantages to paying attention to our bodies to the best of our abilities, why do so many of us spend varying amounts of our time ignoring one or more of our senses? Common reasons why we tend to be less aware of our bodies are discussed in the upcoming chapter.

What Does It Mean To Be Body Aware?--Questions to consider
What changes occur in your body when you are in a stressful situation? Stomach pain? Tight shoulders? Headache? Which of your five senses (sight, hearing, touch, taste and smell) do you rely on the most? Which do you notice the least?

☐Examples Of Reduced Body Awareness
Most of us are not fully aware of our body 100% of the time. In many situations though, being unaware of our physical well-being and how we are moving can result in unnecessary accidents and injuries. Here are a few of the circumstances that can lead to a reduced level of body awareness. Notice which, if any, of these situations are common for you or people you are care about.

Lost in thought, fantasy or planning-
Sometimes we become so immersed in our thoughts, worries, dreams and creative ideas that we lose track of what our body is doing. How often are we driving a car while thinking about what to buy in the grocery store or how we want to respond when we get angry at our boss at work? Artists, inventors, scholars and other creative types are famous for being absorbed in their thoughts and therefore "absent-minded" about what is happening around them. People who have this habit often refer to themselves as being "spacey," "clumsy" or "accident prone".

Sleep deprivation--
Not getting enough high quality rest is an epidemic problem in these fast-paced times. Some of us are so busy that we literally have not scheduled enough time to sleep. Other people have enough hours in the day or night, but are plagued with problems that prevent sleeping deeply: insomnia, restless leg syndrome, sleep apnea or chronic pain. Others stay awake because they feel anxious or are

worrying about the challenges in their life. Poor sleep dulls all of our senses, lowers our energy level and makes it harder to function well, both physically and emotionally.

Multi-tasking--
Walk down the street and notice how many people are using their cell phones, reading or texting, instead of paying attention to where they are going. These days we are so absorbed with multi-tasking that we are willing to walk into traffic without looking, fall over a crack in the sidewalk or bump into and potentially injure the people around us. Unfortunately, we do the same things, only at higher speed, while driving.

We want to eat, drink, argue or chat with friends, check how we look in the mirror, finish a work or school assignment and look for our missing keys or wallet while driving, walking or going down stairs. Instead of doing many things poorly at the same time, we would be better off doing one task carefully at a time, then moving skillfully on to our next activity!

Under the influence of: drugs (including prescription), alcohol or even high amounts of caffeine or sugar--
Any time we alter how our bodies take in and process information from our senses, we change our interaction with the world around us.

Alcohol and many types of drugs can reduce our ability to concentrate and move carefully, which makes driving and other physical tasks more risky. Even high amounts of caffeine or sugar can over stimulate our nervous system causing shaky hands, irritability, mood swings or restlessness. We have to be aware of how these chemicals function in our bodies so we can stay as safe and free of negative consequences as possible.

In pain and trying to ignore it--
Whether we are experiencing pain due to a sudden injury or long-term chronic suffering, our attention is often drawn to part of our bodies that are hurting. It is common to feel we need to ignore

physical discomfort in order to continue functioning in our daily lives.

A person whose hands or back hurt while working may be so concerned with keeping their job or meeting a deadline that they ignore the signs it is time for them to take a break in order to reduce further injury. Someone exercising or playing sports may notice that they twisted an ankle or knee and yet be so determined to finish a workout, race or game that they continue being active despite their worsening condition.

Folks with on-going pain like arthritis, migraine headaches, fibromyalgia or spinal problems may choose to ignore their discomfort in order to continue with the daily activities necessary in their lives. The problem with ignoring the negative experiences in the body is that this lack of attention to detail can reduce response time to potential hazards, could lead to new accidents or worsen current injuries.

Desire to ignore one's body due to feelings of shame, embarrassment or

**as a response to physical or
emotional trauma --**
With varying degrees of severity,
sometimes emotional experiences can
lead to a lack of body awareness. We
may have been criticized, picked on,
bullied or made to feel ashamed of our
bodies. Survivors of rape, sexual
abuse, torture and other forms of
trauma may have disconnected from
feelings altogether.

It is possible we may not pay attention
our bodies due to shyness or lack of
confidence. Certain postures like
holding the shoulders forward,
slouching or looking downward can
become habitual.

When our head and eyes are focused
downward, there is less visual
information about what is happening
around us. If our shoulders are
forward, it becomes harder to breathe
deeply which could reduce our energy
level and ability to feel powerful.

We all deserve to live fully and with
confidence, enjoying ourselves and

knowing we have a right to use the space we occupy with our bodies.

Strong emotions: especially anger, shock, sadness or fear--
During times of strong emotional response our bodies are reacting in various ways. When angry, we tend to have a lot of energy and tension in our muscles, often with a desire to move physically. Anger may lead us to have a desire to attack someone or something.

A shock could be related to physical movement, like having an accident or a sudden change in circumstances like hearing bad news about someone we care about. After an unexpected incident, we may be unable to concentrate well as we try to integrate the new information about what has just happened.

With sadness, there's a tendency to have very low energy and become somewhat numb physically. When we are sad, our muscles often get softer as our heavy emotions pull us away from focus on our bodies and physical movement.

With fear we pay less attention to basic needs, like hunger and thirst, as the body prepares itself to respond to an emergency situation. Even if the source of fear is an ongoing concern like possible layoffs at work or concern over a loved one, our bodies are preparing to fight, run away or freeze depending on our personality type.

Lessening of the senses (sight, hearing, touch, taste and smell) due to the aging process or injury-- Changes that occur to our bodies over time can be especially difficult to notice since they may be shifting very slowly. If our hearing is in decline, we may be less able to hear an oncoming car or other sound that indicates that we could be in danger. When the sense of smell decreases for example, we may not notice the smell of food burning on the stove or gas leaking from a heater.

Most importantly if we are used to a higher level of functioning and tend to trust our instincts, we need to know that the amount or accuracy of the information we are receiving from our senses has changed. Ideally we should have our hearing and vision tested regularly, especially if friends or loved ones are noticing changes in our behavior.

There are many tools available to help us stay safe and high functioning! We can use a cane or walker, glasses or hearing aids, brighter lighting, keep pathways in our home clear and add hand railings to keep ourselves active and independent for as long as possible.

Examples Of Reduced Body Awareness--Questions to consider
Do any of these examples of reduced body awareness seem common in your life? Can you remember times, perhaps in childhood, when you felt more comfortable with your body and movement?

3 Steps to Success, A Fall Reduction Technique

One of the most common ways that people become injured is by falling. Here is a simple way to reduce the likelihood of falls and accidents that I call: 3 Steps to Success.

Any time you are getting ready to walk, and especially if you have been sitting or lying down for a long period, try these moves to prepare yourself to walk safely.

Step One: Warm up and stretch the muscles of your body while you are still sitting down. Gently lengthen your arms and legs, make careful circles with your wrists and ankles and move your spine in a comfortable manner to make sure that your whole body is ready to begin walking.

Step Two: Stand up slowly while keeping the back of your legs in contact with whatever bed, sofa, or chair you have been sitting on. If you are near a wall, railing or other stable item you can hold on to that additional surface for extra support.

If you are using a cane or walker for assistance, reach for it at this time.

Stand up completely until you are as tall as you are able to become, with your shoulders relaxed, chest open and chin in a neutral position. Once you are in this tall and secure way of standing, ask yourself, "Am I dizzy? Do I feel ready to walk?"

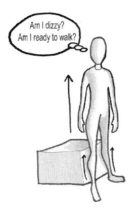

If you are dizzy or lightheaded, either sit back down and relax for a while or continue standing until the dizziness passes with the back of your legs in contact with the item you been sitting on for extra stability.

Step Three: When you are ready to begin walking safely, step forward with confidence! Be proud of yourself for taking these extra few moments to stand up and begin walking with care.

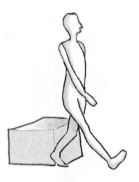

3 Steps to Success--Fall Reduction Technique--Questions to consider

What are at least two changes that would make your home or office safer?

Are the walkways clear of wires and other items that could cause a fall? Can you add a non-slip carpet or mat to your kitchen or bathroom?

Recovering From Loss

Does Time Heal All Wounds?
A traditional expression commonly used in an attempt to console people going through sadness or disappointment is: "Time heals all wounds." Is it true that with no additional effort just because time has passed a person will feel 'healed' from: losing a pet or person they love, romantic break up or career setback?

In many circumstances, the passage of time alone is not likely to help us become stronger. It does not really count as 'grieving time' if we spend it pushing ourselves through busy days of responsibilities and caregiving for others. Unless we give ourselves the attention and healing we need following a loss, months and years may pass when we 'function', but in a fog and not at our full, vibrant capacity.

For today's busy world and our frantic styles of multi-tasking, taking time to pause and prioritize our own needs so we can heal from losses more successfully is a revolutionary process.

Here is a typical scenario. When someone loses their parent or other loved one these days there is often a rush of confusing and upsetting activity before and afterward: Visits to hospitals, tough medical decisions, complicated legal and financial paperwork, a funeral to plan, supporting other loved ones and friends of the deceased, clearing out and dividing up the person's belongings.

At the end of this huge, difficult marathon of activities, many of us find that we have fallen behind on our other life responsibilities. Perhaps even a few days after the death of someone we care about or other major life change, we are scrambling around trying to catch up on missed work, to focus on money challenges or to care for our own health problems. Almost completely missing is time to gently reflect on what has happened and begin to explore ways to feel better.

While developing Body Aware Grieving, I have found that the types of mourning that truly lead to feeling better are more active than passive. By "active" I do not necessarily mean moving around physically. I am talking about making conscious choices about how we can spend our time in ways that ultimately bring us relief from the pain of a specific loss. We can learn to grieve more skillfully.

Does Time Heal All Wounds?-- Questions to consider

How many hours per week are you willing to devote to your personal care and healing? Can you put these self-care times in your calendar and honor them as a high priority, making sure they do not get easily cancelled or postponed?

Do you still feel affected by a loss that was never given any attention?

When Will I Be Over This?

One of the biggest questions while experiencing sadness and frustration over a loss is, "When will I be over this?" For a person experiencing grief it seems natural to want to go back to the way one felt before. In many cases though, when a life event had been dramatic enough, people actually go on to become a different version of the person they were before.

Instead of expecting ourselves to get "over" an important change like losing a job, loved one or romance, it is possible to realize we are now in a different phase of life. With some challenges, it is easy to see which new life skills one is developing. Other experiences are so traumatic or painful that just our ability to endure and move forward is in itself a wonderful accomplishment.

We need to learn how to care for our hurting bodies and minds after a difficult loss or disappointment. We can create personalized grieving systems that help us feel better.

With proper attention to our own needs, we can become more than 'healed' after a loss. In many cases, we can become stronger, smarter, more appreciative and empathetic compared to our previous selves!

After a major life change, you are not the same person you used to be. Try not to put too much pressure on yourself. Day by day, you are already in the natural process of transition and development. Allow yourself time to let this new person you are becoming emerged. It is possible you will end up better than you were before in ways that you cannot currently predict.

When Will I Be Over This?-- Questions to consider

Are there parts of your current situation that you must, however sadly, now accept? What skills, memories, relationships and wisdom did this person or experience bring into your life that you can take with you and continue to develop over time?

What is Grief?

It is not easy to define grief since there are many different causes of emotional pain and beliefs about how to lessen feelings of loss and longing. A dictionary definition of Grief is: Intense emotional suffering caused by loss, disaster, misfortune; acute sorrow or deep sadness. The words grief and mourning are often used in a similar manner to each other.

Often grief includes a period of experimentation and learning. Our body and mind are searching for ways to feel better after a loss, shock or disappointment.

People going through transition often wonder, "When will I feel like myself again? How can I adjust to life without the person or activity I am missing?" Grief can be a questioning process which often includes a search to understand what has happened. What are the facts? Has a parent died? Did a job or career end? Has a marriage or other important relationship changed?

While grief is most commonly associated with the death of a loved one, people may have strong feelings of sadness, longing or remembrance after a romantic breakup, period of life that has passed, career or financial change, life goal that no longer seems within reach or conflict with a friend or family member.

Many people think that "grieving" means you will stay stuck in dark and sad times. Actually the very opposite can be true! The main benefit of taking time to acknowledge and adjust to an important loss or challenge is to be able to move on to other opportunities even more vibrantly, with deeper and renewed appreciation for the enjoyments of life. After a struggle or difficulty, the good times in life may be even sweeter.

What is Grief?--Questions to consider
If you are going through a difficult transition, can you look for ways to be extra kind to yourself? Instead of telling yourself what to do and how to feel throughout each day, can you ask, "What do I need right now? How can I reduce the amount of pressure I am feeling and begin to console and comfort myself?"

Goals For Skillful Grieving

It is important to understand that there is no 'right' or 'wrong' way to grieve. Even for those of us who are experienced at making it through hard times, painful or sad feelings may be intense and part of our lives during and after a major life change.

'Skillful grieving' is the ability to approach a painful topic or life change in a way that helps us feel better and not worse afterwards.

In order to become more skillful at grieving we can learn to:

***Find ways to balance the daily responsibilities in our lives with the additional time we will need for self-care during and after a loss

***Keep our health as stable as possible by reducing the likelihood of avoidable accidents and injuries, stress based illnesses or misuse of food, alcohol, drugs

***Discover which forms of commemoration we personally find

most healing. No two people or losses are alike.

***Minimize repeated feelings of regret, guilt or shame by realizing we can only change the present and our own behavior in the future.

***Understand that receiving guidance or assistance during a hard time can mean we are being wise, not 'weak'

***Identify when we need to request help from potential caregivers, professionals or organizations

***Learn how to reduce the amount of the influence a problem in one part of our lives has on our relationships, finances, personal goals and health.

The biggest challenge to skillful grieving in this day and age is that people are so busy! For most of us it is not possible to stop the rest of our activities and responsibilities for months at a time, in order to fully adjust to an important change. What it means to grieve in a satisfying manner will be different now than other times in history. We will need to invent new rituals and ways of connecting with one another that work well in our current lifestyles.

Goals for Skillful Grieving--Questions to consider

Are you ready to release a regret? Is there something you wish you had done differently? Would you like to be compassionate with yourself and say: "I tried my best under the circumstances and I cannot change the past. If necessary I will make different choices about how I behave in the future."?

5 Grief Time Savers

Experiences like loss of a loved one or pet, dealing with an illness, going through a romantic break-up or stress about money can be even more upsetting when the process seems to lack structure and guidance. Hopefully understanding these suggestions about grief and transition can help us save time, and perhaps a bit of pain, as we each discover our own ways to begin healing.

1) We can reduce our responsibilities as much as possible during sad times.

If we are going through a difficult experience, we will need as much time and energy as possible to devote to our self-care and healing. It is smart, not "selfish" to temporarily minimize the amount of stress we are dealing with each day. We can look at our calendars and cancel or postpone as many non-urgent activities as possible. **If we treat ourselves well now, we will be able to skillfully resume our roles as a caregiver, employee, partner or parent more quickly.**

2) We can understand that we all need help sometimes.

It is possible to be an independent and strong person, while still accepting and even asking for help. Friends, family, co-workers, caregiving or religious organizations, online or local communities may be willing and able to make our current journey less painful. Often it can take an event like a severe injury or illness before we realize that literally no one can take excellent care of themselves in all circumstances. **If we don't waste our energy fighting or ignoring a problem, we will have more time and strength available to improve our current situation.**

3) We can be patient with ourselves and each other.

For traumatic and confusing events, we may want, and need, a long time to comprehend what has happened. My father had been blessed with excellent health his whole life until diagnosed with cancer at age 70. I had not yet adjusted to his being sick and soon had to accept that he had died.

One of the few relaxing moments before, during or after his funeral was when I told myself, "It is OK. My father will be dead for the rest of my life. I can take as long as I need to adjust to the changes that are taking place right now." **Healing can continue throughout our lifetime and current losses will likely look and feel different as we grow and change with time.**

4) We can expect the unexpected from ourselves and people around us.

Under extreme levels of stress, people can behave in surprising ways that may be either very uplifting or disappointing. Perhaps a person we thought was dependable responds in an unreliable or insensitive manner right when we most need them. It is also possible that someone new or unexpected steps forward in a very caring and supportive way.

In stressful times, the best and worst of each of us may be exposed. When tensions are high family, friends and communities may either cooperate in a loving way or become torn apart by fighting. **We may be surprised by the behavior of people we thought we knew well or our own response and abilities during an emergency. Unexpected offerings of assistance may come from strangers or casual friends.**

5) When someone has been sick a long time, it still can be surprising

when they actually die. Caregivers can spend months or years caring for a loved one who is ailing. That quiet moment when they are no longer with us may still be quite shocking. Especially if a person we have been caring for has survived many potentially fatal health problems before, it can be hard to get used to their being gone.

A similar feeling of surprise can accompany other life changes, even if they have been predicted like leaving a job, a romantic breakup, children growing up and becoming more independent or changes in lifestyle due to aging. **Preparing for a change is not the same as when it actually happens, we need to give ourselves the opportunity to adjust to each new phase in life.**

5 Grief Time Savers--Questions to consider
Would you like to add your own ideas to this list? What advice would you offer someone who is going through a challenge similar to your own? Have

you found ways to invent healing
rituals during times of sadness?

Getting Stronger

GETTING STRONGER

What is Commemoration?
It is important to understand the differences between "grieving" a loss and "commemorating" a person's life and influence. Grief and mourning generally refer to the often painful initial phase of getting used to a major life change that has happened, like the death of a loved one or pet.

Commemoration can be more focused on who we have become as a result of the experiences we have had and people we have known. The process of commemoration can occur long after an individual has passed away or important phase of life has been completed. Hopefully, over time we will be able to look at photos, or remember favorite memories about a person or time in our life that has passed and appreciate what we have enjoyed and learned.

To me, being able to commemorate, rather than "mourn" is like a reward for having made it further along in the process of grieving. Instead of being focused as much on the past, "commemoration" is more about who we have become today. It can be empowering to consider, "In what ways am I wiser, stronger and more skillful because this person or experience has been part of my life?" "Which activities can I choose that would make a loved one proud of who I am continuing to become?"

When we have had relationships that were complicated or even hateful, we can still use the time after they have passed to grow and improve. In cases like these, over time we may have fewer feelings of anger or fear and instead perhaps a sense of relief that they are gone. We can even "commemorate" transitions that were extremely difficult to endure like various types of abuse or trauma, divorce or bankruptcy. Some experiences may have been so difficult, that we can be proud of ourselves just to have survived!

When the initial shock of living without a person, pet or phase of life wears off, it can become easier to look back on times, both good and bad, more clearly. It is a process of seeing less of what we have lost, and more of how much we can do with what we have been given.

What is commemoration?--Questions to consider
What activity or goal appeals to you that would have made a person you are missing proud of you? Can you think of three or more times in your life when you felt very happy?

Memories and Moving Forward
After a disappointment, people often try to "cheer themselves up" almost immediately. It is really a delicate balance to find the right amount of time and attention to spend thinking about life's sadder experiences. Too much emphasis on the darker moments could potentially lead to feeling "stuck" in those thoughts. However, the risks of trying to ignore powerful life changes like the death of a person or pet who has been important to us is also worth considering.

Have you ever felt like you were about to sneeze and then waited for it, but it did not arrive? There is a sense of anticipation and tension during the moments building up to a big sneeze. Doesn't it feel so much more relaxing after you actually sneeze? Grieving can be the same way.

This story about memories, memorials and moving forward is from my own life. My sister Shelley died on August 7th 2008, a few days after her 40th birthday. As is often the case after losing a loved one, the first year following her death I floated along in a haze. It was like being tired for a whole year and everything seemed kind of gray. As much as possible I tried to keep my responsibilities to a minimum and "gave in" to being really sad.

After many months of leading a quieter lifestyle, much of my enthusiasm and motivation to be active came back–bit by bit. Slowly, my appetite returned and I had the desire and energy to get back into doing activities I enjoy again. By the end of the second year without my sister, I'd begun to feel more energetic, happy and focused on exciting new projects.

Then as the second anniversary of Shelley's death was coming up, I started to consider what I should do to commemorate this important date in my family's life when one of my friends made an interesting comment. She said, "I have not had anyone really close to me pass away yet, so this may sound naive, but why do people make themselves so miserable around the date when someone has died?" It was a perfect question.

The answer I gave is, "When you have a very deep loss, the feeling of misery can remain just below the surface of your skin indefinitely. Finding ways to remember these important people, especially around a memorial, birthday or other special date can actually relieve a bit of this pain by letting it come to the surface and be expressed.

As the date of my sister's death approached, I began to be flooded with intense thoughts and memories about her and my own journey of recovery since her passing. Trying to ignore her memorial on August 7th would be like needing to sneeze and getting frozen that way. On August 8th, 9th and 10th I would still feel just as uncomfortable. Instead, I chose to organize a gathering in her honor.

On the day of my sister's memorial, ten of her friends and family members met in front of the apartment where she had lived in San Francisco. It was hard to be in front of her home without her.

Together we all hiked to the top of one of the tallest hills in Golden Gate Park, a beautiful place that had always been very special to her.

We told stories about Shelley, looked at some pictures of her we had brought and talked about how the first two years without her had been for each of us. We compared which activities, moments and locations had reminded us of Shelley throughout the past year. After a few minutes of shared silence, we left a large bouquet of flowers at the base of a huge tree.

Then, we walked back out of the park to enjoy a dinner together at one of the many fabulous restaurants in San Francisco. Expecting that we might still be feeling very sad, we had reserved the most private table available. By then though, our collective mood had started to lift, we had all started to feel lighter and more energetic. When the meal arrived we were mostly chatting about other parts of our lives and work. By dessert we were joking and laughing. Our memorial gathering had been a 'success' because we found ways to think about a person we were missing in a manner that helped us feel better afterward.

Creating meaningful rituals, sharing our feelings with friends or family and allowing for times to remember people and experiences that have been important to us is skillful grieving. Learning to do it in a way that best suits our personal needs can lead to a sense of satisfaction, relief and a readiness to move on to more joyful experiences. **It can be healing and empowering to realize that it is** possible to remember the past, live in the present and plan for the future all at the same time.

Memories and Moving Forward-- Questions to consider

What dates on the calendar remind you of an important person or life change (birthdays, memorials, anniversaries, holidays)? Would you like to use these special days as an opportunity to acknowledge how those people and experiences have influenced who you have become?

7 Ways to Become More Resilient

What is the difference between a person who becomes despondent or even suicidal when faced with painful losses and someone who remains determined to keep moving forward in life? How can we learn to overcome obstacles while maintaining an optimistic attitude?

To answer these questions, I look to the wisdom of senior citizens. No matter what they have been through, the fact that they have persevered long enough to become older proves they have a willingness to keep going.

According to the dictionary, 'resilient' is: the tendency to recover from or adjust more easily to misfortune or change. One of my favorite and most inspiring examples of a person who is resilient is my personal fitness training client and friend Mildred, who is 102 years old and blind. She spends most of her time in bed but her mind is still functioning perfectly.

Mildred epitomizes having a strong "will to live" despite the many setbacks and challenges she faces. She and I have talked extensively about what it takes to become resilient. Here are the main ways she has sustained herself so long with specific examples:

1) Being versatile and grateful
Mildred has lost her vision over the past few years and is now legally blind. Of course, this is hugely disappointing to her, but she finds ways to savor her other senses. She loves to enjoy the taste, shape and smells of her favorite

foods. When Mildred goes outside on the patio near her room, she takes in the fresher air with huge deep breaths and talks about how the sun and breeze feel on her skin.

2) Having a supportive network of friends and family

For each birthday, Mildred's daughters organize a huge party where relatives and friends come to honor and celebrate with her. She looks forward to these parties and each of the other holidays the family shares together for months in advance.

Not all of us choose to marry or have children like Mildred. Regardless of our family circumstances, we each need to cultivate important relationships. We need to care for others and be taken care of. We can stay close to people we grew up with, find new friendships to develop or participate in group activities or religious organizations. **Being part of a community is vital for most people's well being.**

3) A sense of humor

A few years ago, Mildred had a major setback and new injuries when an attendant who cleaned her bathroom left the toilet seat up. Because of her poor vision, she was unable to see that the seat had been left up, and she fell in. She did not have enough strength to get herself back out easily, as a result of previous shoulder injury. After some panic and struggle, she got herself out of the bathroom and was able to tell the story and laugh. She joked, "I sure did not come this far just to die in a toilet! That can be someone else's story!" **Especially during hard situations, finding a way to laugh and see any amount of humor can help sustain us.**

4) Believing in a greater power

When she was 85 years old, Mildred was seriously injured in a grocery store when some careless teens hit her accidentally with their shopping cart. I am fascinated by what sustained her through the surgery and a year of painful rehabilitation sessions that followed. She understood that at her age recovery would be slow and possibly not very complete.

When I asked how she got through that time, Mildred replied, "If God had wanted me already, he would have taken me then." Mildred happens to have a specific religious background and draws support and guidance from her beliefs. **Even for those of us who do not feel attracted to a particular faith or religion, it could be comforting for us to find some type of greater power that we feel is helping us through tough times.**

5) Choosing one's thoughts carefully
While she does not completely avoid thinking about loved ones who have passed away, medical and health problems or personal dramas, Mildred is very careful about how long she lets herself dwell on negative and sad images. With any type of potentially upsetting topic, Mildred is very clear with herself and whomever she is talking with when it is time to stop focusing on a disturbing idea. **Sometimes when we are upset it can relieve stress to focus on more**

neutral or uplifting thoughts for a while.

6) Having realistic expectations
Many of us will look at a person who is living under difficult circumstances and perhaps ask, "How can they live like that?" Sometimes when I observe how frail Mildred's body has become and how many of her favorite activities and hobbies she no longer is capable of doing, I marvel at how she still maintains a positive attitude.

Before every workout together, I phone her to confirm our fitness session. Occasionally she spends a few minutes complaining about how much pain she is in, and then she always says: "Well, we will just have to do what we can!" Mildred wastes very little time comparing her current situation to the past, or planning too far into the future. She is willing to work hard in any way she needs to in order to make each day beneficial. **We can only do our best, where we are, with what we have.**

7) Taking opportunities to not miss bliss

Mildred knows how to savor pleasure in a way that is amazing! I bring her roses to smell and she inhales the beautiful fragrance and asks what other plants are in the garden, how bright the colors are and if they are growing quickly.

When Mildred eats a piece of chocolate, she savors it by rolling each small piece in her mouth. She talks about how smooth it feels and which happy memories she is reminded of while eating it.

Though it is hard physically for her to move and she can no longer stand or walk on her own, Mildred loves stretching her body and asks visitors to gently massage her hands or comb her hair. She has lost many of the advantages of being youthful, yet enjoys impressing people who respect how well her mind works at age 102 and she loves making jokes, singing and asking about recent events in the news. Mildred is a master of a Don't Miss Bliss lifestyle!

7 Ways to Become More Resilient--Questions to consider

Who do you know who seems to have a positive attitude about life? What questions would you like to ask that person? Can you think of a problem or challenge that was really difficult and remember what you did to help yourself through it?

Healing with Cultures and Religions from Around the World

We don't have to be limited by what we know from our own culture, family or religious belief. It is possible to explore other options and experiment with a ritual or habit from another community if it appeals to you.

People have been having hard times since the beginning of history and in every corner of the world. For just as long, people have searched for ways to feel better during and after every type of loss. There is a huge variety of styles of healing to learn from.

Many Spanish speaking countries celebrate an event called Day of the

Dead. These are festivals filled with colors, music, costumes and dancing! Mourners from any culture may find that dramatic, artistic public system of commemoration very appealing. Some Asian cultures know more about the benefits of meditation and the value of finding enough quiet and solitude. Notice which styles of grieving and renewal appeals to your current mood and needs.

You do not have to be from these places, or even travel there in person, to borrow aspects of each type of wisdom. Feel free to read books, watch movies or connect with a community or culture that you are attracted to either in person or online.

Uniformly all religions have tried to address suffering and recovery in different ways. When I look at who I've seen go through hard times, the people who I have known and respected who are somewhat religious, regardless of what their specific belief is, seem to have found a sense of peace and strength more easily.

We can turn towards all the religions with a respectful and curious attitude and ask, "What ideas or advice do they have that is special and could benefit me right now?" You do not need to join any particular group or religion, nor do you need to agree with everything they do or believe, to find parts of their philosophy or rituals beneficial.

It is possible to approach various religious or cultural organizations and see who is most welcoming and interested in helping you. The more we respect each other and learn from one another, the greater the range of healing tools we can all choose from.

Healing with Cultures and Religions From Around the World--Questions to consider

What countries, cultures, or religions have you been curious to explore?
Have you ever had a problem and help came from a person or activity that was very unexpected?

More Body Aware Grieving Resources

I'm glad to offer additional Body Aware Grieving information and healing tools!

In the blog section of www.BodyAwareGrieving.com there are articles and audio podcasts on a wide range of topics, including additional healing techniques.

Subscribe to the BodyAwareGrieving.com website if you would like to be notified by email when live events, webinars, my upcoming radio show, books, exercise videos and other products become available.

I can be reached by email using the "contact" link on the Body Aware Grieving website if you have interest in consulting, media requests, collaboration with your organization or business and discounts on books for professional use with clients, non-profits and caregiving services.

Quantity sales. Special discounts are

available on quantity purchases by corporations, associations, and others. For details, contact the publisher at:

Attn: Margo Rose
PHT Press
29 Orinda Way, Suite 881
Orinda, Ca 94563

Or by email via the contact link at www.BodyAwareGrieving.com

I also love to connect with people on Facebook at:
facebook.com/BodyAwareGrieving
and on Twitter at:
www.Twitter.com/BodyAwareGrief

Best wishes,
Margo Rose

Special Thanks

One of the most important sources of inspiration in creating Body Aware Grieving is the hospice community that helped care for my family when both my mother and father were passing away. Their calm, kind, knowledgeable advice and practical services made those hard times much easier and less scary.

The first time I realized that a book could be immediately useful in caring for our health during stressful experiences is the classic guide by Louise Hay, *You Can Heal Your Life*. Her book encourages each reader to feel they have the power to improve their circumstances, and I try to inspire a similar confidence with this book.

The caring and wise community at www.Breema.com has helped guide me with their *9 Principles of Harmony* and comfort-based styles of movement and bodywork.

In the many years it has taken to turn my personal experiences into a new career I have consistently asked

Allison Bliss, www.AllisonBliss.com for her excellent advice about business, marketing and communication. Allison Bliss helps me understand what steps to take to turn creative ideas into a successful business.

Nicole Robinson believed in my ideas early on and shared her time, energy and organizational skills to help develop the BodyAwareGrieving.com website and content.

Beth Barany, www.BethBarany.com is a creativity coach for writers who also specializes in book marketing for authors. When writing a whole book seemed overwhelming to me, Beth was able to break the process down into simple achievable steps.

Cover design, layout and experienced guidance about self publishing have been provided by Lisa Dalton, www.LisaDalton.net. As well, Lisa's tough yet tender style of life coaching was essential in helping pull this project into completion.

Sheila Sheridan has been an English instructor and writer for many years. She has provided exceptional support and is the primary editor of this book.

Tracie Clayton-Hom has been a grief counselor for over 10 years. I deeply appreciate how she has shared her valuable wisdom, editing and proofreading suggestions.

For mentorship and inspiration, I thank radio show host, and caregiver advocate Carolyn Brent of www.caregiverstory.com.

My brother Dr. Barry Rotman, MD has offered his advice about the name of this book and ways to create a healing guide that would be useful for doctors to share with their patients.

Much appreciation to Simone Rotman, my niece, who created the beautiful, custom illustrations shown in the 3 Steps to Success chapter.

Amazing bodywork healers have helped me recover from various injuries over the years and kept me feeling athletic and functional.

Lifelong gratitude to:
Alexandra Kaufman,
www.ManualMedicine.info

Kevin Minney,
www.KevinMinney.com

Dr. Sue Mullen, DC
www.GoodLifeBerkeley.com

When I wanted to create a silent writing retreat in a beautiful, natural setting, two facilities generously offered to host me.

If you are looking for a peaceful, healing environment in the Northern California area check out:
Ananda Meditation Retreat Center,
www.MeditationRetreat.org
and
Silent Stay Retreat Hermitage,
www.SilentStay.com

My fitness client and friend Mildred Taylor has generously shared her wisdom about life and how to live with passion for over 100 years. Thanks as well to her daughters Judy and Nancy, who have lovingly assisted Mildred on her long journey.

For their constant encouragement and support through every type of personal life challenge and celebration I acknowledge with gratitude my longtime friends:
Emily, Francie, Judy, Tracy, Julie, Zandra, Billium, Jennifer and Rita.

With much appreciation I also thank my beloved life partner, Patricia, and her beautiful family for believing in me more deeply than I knew was possible.

Your Healing Action Plan

This is the part of the book, where you are welcome to begin creating your own Healing Action Plan!

Which parts of Body Aware Grieving seem the most interesting and useful to you? Feel free to look at the *questions to consider* at the end of each section and answer any of them that you find intriguing in the extra pages provided here.

I have also listed the 10 Actions of Healing in hopes that you will be inspired to invent your own examples of activities that you would like to try. The more ideas you generate for each area that interests you, the better!

This area can also be used as a personal journal if you want to add photos, quotes or your own writing. Most of all, I hope you congratulate yourself for being willing to experiment with new ways to help yourself learn and grow, even during challenging times.

10 Actions of Healing

Hibernate
Can you improve the quality or quantity of rest you are getting?

Hydrate
Are you taking in enough healthy fluids and juicy foods?

Commemorate
What or whom are you missing now?

Create
Can you express your feelings with art, music, writing or movement?

Liberate
Which old ideas or items are no longer necessary?

Donate
Can you help others in a way that is uplifting to you?

Celebrate
How can you have more fun and enjoyment?

Relate
Who is currently most caring and helpful?

Contemplate Fate
What has the most meaning to you?

Rejuvenate
Who can you become now?

How much time is needed for each 'action'?

- 5-15 Minutes
- 1-5 Hours
- 1 Day
- 10 or more Days
- Ongoing

Also customize each idea by taking note of how much it might cost:

- Free
- Under $25
- $25-$100
- Over $100

As well, consider with whom you may want to share each activity:

- Alone
- Friends or family
- A romantic partner
- Your pet or other animal
- Groups of people who share your interests, either in person or online
- Religious organizations
- Professional providers

10 ACTIONS OF HEALING: HIBERNATE

How can you improve the quantity or quality of the rest you get?

5-15 minutes	COST	WHO
1 - 5 hours		
1 day		
10+ days		
Ongoing		

10 ACTIONS OF HEALING: HYDRATE

Are you taking in enough healthy fluids and juicy foods?

5-15 minutes	COST	WHO
1 - 5 hours		
1 day		
10+ days		
Ongoing		

10 ACTIONS OF HEALING: COMMEMORATE

What or whom are you missing now?

5-15 minutes	COST	WHO
1 - 5 hours		
1 day		
10+ days		
Ongoing		

10 ACTIONS OF HEALING: CREATE

Can you express your feelings with art, music, writing or movement?

5-15 minutes	COST	WHO
1 - 5 hours		
1 day		
10+ days		
Ongoing		

10 ACTIONS OF HEALING: LIBERATE

Which old ideas are no longer necessary?

5-15 minutes	COST	WHO
1 - 5 hours		
1 day		
10+ days		
Ongoing		

10 ACTIONS OF HEALING: DONATE

Can you help others in a way that is uplifting to you?

5-15 minutes	COST	WHO
1 - 5 hours		
1 day		
10+ days		
Ongoing		

10 ACTIONS OF HEALING: CELEBRATE

How can you have more fun and enjoyment?

5-15 minutes	COST	WHO
1 - 5 hours		
1 day		
10+ days		
Ongoing		

10 ACTIONS OF HEALING: RELATE

Who is currently most caring and helpful?

5-15 minutes	COST	WHO
1 - 5 hours		
1 day		
10+ days		
Ongoing		

10 ACTIONS OF HEALING: CONTEMPLATE FATE

What has the most meaning to you?

5-15 minutes	COST	WHO
1 - 5 hours		
1 day		
10+ days		
Ongoing		

10 ACTIONS OF HEALING: REJUVINATE

Who can you become now?

5-15 minutes	COST	WHO
1 - 5 hours		
1 day		
10+ days		
Ongoing		

Here are the questions from the end of each chapter. You can answer as many or few of them as you find interesting and beneficial.

Part 1: Protecting Your Health

Knowing When We Need Help-- Questions to consider

What is the most challenging part of your day? Why? Can you think of two people or organizations that may be able to make this current problem easier?

3 Types of Injury Reduction-- Questions to consider

What is one change you are willing to make that could help reduce your chances of injury? Make a list of five or more activities that you find calming and enjoyable, that can be done in 10 minutes. Can you do at least two of these activities each day for a week and see how you feel?

What Does It Mean To Be Body Aware?--Questions to consider

What changes occur in your body when you are in a stressful situation? Stomach pain? Tight shoulders? Headache? Which of your five senses (sight, hearing, smell, touch, taste) do you rely on the most? Which do you notice the least?

Examples Of Reduced Body Awareness--Questions to consider

Do any of these examples of reduced body awareness seem common in your life? Can you remember times, perhaps in childhood, when you felt more comfortable with your body and movement?

3 Steps to Success--Fall Reduction Technique--Questions to consider

What are at least two changes that would make your home or office safer? Are the walkways clear of wires and other items that could cause a fall? Can you add a non-slip carpet or mat to your kitchen or bathroom?

Part 2: Recovering From Loss

Does Time Heal All Wounds?--
Questions to consider

How many hours per week are you willing to devote to your personal care and healing? Can you put these self-care times in your calendar and honor them as a high priority, making sure they do not get easily cancelled or postponed? Do you still feel affected by a loss that was never given any attention?

When Will I Be Over This?-- Questions to consider

Are there parts of your current situation that you must, however sadly, now accept? What skills, memories, relationships and wisdom did this person or experience bring into your life that can you take with you and continue to develop over time?

What is Grief?--Questions to consider

If you are already going through a difficult transition, can you find ways to be extra kind to yourself? Instead of telling yourself what to do and how to feel throughout each day, can you find more opportunities to ask, "What do I need right now? How can I reduce the amount of pressure I am feeling and begin to console and comfort myself?"

Goals for Skillful Grieving--Questions to consider

Are you ready to release a regret? Is there something you wish you had done differently? Can you be compassionate with yourself right now and say:
"I tried my best under the circumstances and I cannot change the past."

5 Grief Time Savers--Questions to consider

Would you like to add your own ideas to this list? What advice would you offer someone who is going a challenge similar to your own?

Part 3: Getting Stronger

What is commemoration?
What activity or goal appeals to you that would have made a person you are missing proud of you? Can you think of three or more times in your life when you felt very happy?

Memories and Moving Forward-- Questions to consider

What dates on your calendar remind you of an important person or life change (birthdays, memorials, anniversaries, holidays)? Would you like use these special days as an opportunity to acknowledge how those people and experiences have influenced who you have become?

7 Ways to Become More Resilient-- Questions to consider

Who do you know who seems to have a positive attitude about life? What questions would you like to ask that person? Can you think of a problem or challenge that was really difficult and remember what you did to help yourself through it?

Healing with Cultures--

What countries, cultures, or religions have you been curious to explore? Have you ever had a problem and help came from a person or activity that was very unexpected?

Healing Action Plan

The following pages can be used for journaling, photos, quotes and notes:

Healing Action Plan

Healing Action Plan

Healing Action Plan

Healing Action Plan

Healing Action Plan

Healing Action Plan

Healing Action Plan

Healing Action Plan

Healing Action Plan

Healing Action Plan

Healing Action Plan

Healing Action Plan

Healing Action Plan

Made in the USA
Middletown, DE
11 June 2016